FINDING EASY WALKS
Wherever You Are

Also by Marjorie Turner Hollman

Easy Walks in Massachusetts
More Easy Walks in Massachusetts
Easy Walks and Paddles in the Ten Mile River Watershed, Editor

FINDING EASY WALKS
Wherever You Are

Marjorie Turner Hollman

Table of Contents

Foreword

Why do we love the outdoors? It must be a sense of wonder that is so lacking in our screen-filled lives nowadays. The observation of the cycle of life, death, and rebirth. The amazing connection and relationship between water and stone, flora and fauna, bugs, animals and fungi, man and nature. The reminder that we are all part of something greater than ourselves. The serenity of crickets and peeper frogs singing in the night. The beauty of the leaves changing color with the season.

This is why a life-changing illness couldn't keep Marjorie Turner Hollman away from the outdoors. She has made adaptations using hiking poles, ice-cooling scarves, and a cool tandem bicycle she travels on with her husband so she can still experience all of these things.

Her efforts to get outside and write books that help make others feel that they can do so too is truly inspiring. The *Easy Walks in Massachusetts* book series offers useful and informative guides for those who can't or don't want to put on a pack and hike the Appalachian Trail. The books highlight local options that also offer a sense of wonder in their own way.

Finding Easy Walks Wherever You Are further illustrates Marjorie Turner Hollman's curious and adventurous nature and her ability to persuade others to explore. When you get out of the car and off (or even onto) a beaten path you will certainly experience a place in a much different way. Exploring these natural places while traveling or visiting provides the same beauty, stillness, wonder, and serenity, but also the potential to learn even more about this planet we all call home. Even within one state there can be many different ecosystems and organisms that reside there.

This book offers resources, safety tips, true stories, and experiences that will encourage all to get out and find a trail. So what are you waiting for?

Mark Mandeville and Raianne Richards
Founders, Massachusetts Walking Tour, the annual walking concert tour promoting local arts and culture

Introduction

Each time I publish a new *Easy Walks in Massachusetts* trails book, I hear the same question: "How do you find all these trails?" This book is my (extended) answer. Within these pages you'll learn how we discover Easy Walks when we visit a new area, and so much more. Observations come from trails mostly in New England. We have traveled and discovered Easy Walks in various sections of the country, and outside the U.S., but for the most part, our normal outings take place quite near where we live in south central Massachusetts.

In 2011, I began seeking out local trails, first to write about in a series of newspaper articles for the Bellingham Bulletin and later for the creation of what became the first in my *Easy Walks in Massachusetts* trail guide series. Three books later, these guides document more than 130 trails in 37 contiguous towns in south-central Massachusetts.

People seek out Easy Walks for many reasons. You may have small children, or older parents who cannot take on the challenging trails they used to. You, or those you love, may have health issues that preclude venturing onto rocky or rooty trails that present trip hazards. Your children may have special needs, and the outdoors may offer real challenges in keeping them safe. Despite having substantial paralysis in one leg, I have walked all of the trails in my Easy Walks books with support, and continue to seek out Easy Walks wherever we are.

- Chapter One explains the specifics of what makes a trail an Easy Walk. This serves as a checklist for choosing where to go and for trail maintainers.

- Chapter Two describes some of the joys of finding and revisiting Easy Walks as opposed to more challenging trails. There's a lot to enjoy besides just walking!

- Chapter Three provides helpful checklists and shares the lessons we have learned about where to find Easy Walks in an area.

- Chapter Four expands on Chapter Three with specific online and map tools and strategies we have found to be useful for finding Easy Walks.

- Chapter Five discusses basic equipment helpful to your safe and enjoyable outdoors experience.

- Chapter Six provides safety tips and reference material you may find helpful.

- Chapter Seven discusses the unique enjoyment and challenges of multi-use and "rail trails."

- Chapter Eight describes some fun and atypical activities possible on the trail.

- Chapter Nine invokes "Miss Manners" on the trail.

- Chapter Ten is an important primer for all of us, whether dog owners or those who encounter dogs.

- Chapter Eleven encourages you to anticipate trail conditions, with tips for avoiding or handling infrequent surprises that may come up.

- Chapter Twelve outlines the responsibilities and skills that will be helpful when leading others on Easy Walks.

- Chapter Thirteen encourages trail maintainers and builders to consider Easy Walks features that will help make flatter trails more accessible to users with challenges. This technical chapter points to trail features that hinder an Easy Walk, drawing from our own experiences.

The term Easy Walk is capitalized to emphasize the concepts we talk about throughout the book. The pronouns "I" and "we" are used inconsistently. "I" refers specifically to me and my own personal experiences. "We" is used for my shared experiences with many generous friends, hiking buddies, and my husband Jon. May this book help ease your path, offer encouragement, and allow you to avoid some common missteps on the trail. Happy Trails!

Postscript

As we were completing this book in 2020, the world was in the midst of the Covid-19 pandemic. Many have been reducing travel and staying closer to home, yet looking for places to get outdoors. Overcrowding of the most visible trails has created a health hazard. The information in this book may be helpful to those seeking uncrowded locations and new safe adventures.

Part 1
Before Heading Out on an Easy Walk

Chapter 1
Introducing Easy Walks

What is an Easy Walk?

Many enjoy getting outdoors for a relaxing stroll or invigorating walk. For those who cannot or do not wish to undertake steep or difficult hiking trails, Easy Walks will fit the bill for a relaxing walk, an outing with the dog, or a stroll with children or elders. These are outdoor trails and paths that are not too challenging, are reasonably flat, and are hazard-free for those of us with mobility challenges. These are non-motorized vehicular trails and unpaved.

Who benefits from finding an Easy Walk trail?

- Those seeking a relaxing walk in lieu of a rugged hike

- Anyone walking with a baby stroller or using a wheelchair

- Those with physical impairments that limit mobility—whether these are permanent or temporary, resulting from injury, over-use, or other cause (We all face challenges as we age!)

- Those who have been sedentary and wish to become more active

What makes a trail an Easy Walk?

Trails with improved walking surfaces are nearly always Easy Walks. We look for trails with places of interest—often featuring wetlands, views, or history—and not too much elevation change. While a few heavily used Accessible Trails (that is, posted as Handicapped Accessible) may actually be paved with asphalt, most "improved" surfaces are simply those where the surface has been leveled at some

If you see a sign like this, believe it! (photo credit, Kate MacLeod, on the trail in Hawaii)

time in the past. This minimizes roots and rocks to create a smoother foot path. Rail trails with stone dust surfaces make wonderful Easy Walks.

Our challenge is finding subsets of the many unimproved hiking trails and abandoned roads that feature:

- Few or no large rocks, steps, or excessively steep slopes

- A limited number of exposed tree roots that pose trip and balance hazards

- Few or no fallen trees and a minimum of fallen branches and brush

- Manageable vertical and side slopes

- Manageable improvements at obstacles, such as sufficiently wide "bog bridges" in wetlands, or bridges or boardwalks with steps having low rises and handrails

Sometimes we see what looks like a well-used trail branching off, only to find it is a "people trail." This is the unintended result of many walkers or fishermen heading close to a spot of interest, or simply missing a turn. These unimproved trails often peter out and are not Easy Walks.

In my experience, level trails can sometimes be rather boring, but rock scrambling is beyond my physical capabilities. Rough trails filled with rocks and roots are beyond my capabilities as well. Easy Walks lie somewhere between completely level trails and trails that require mostly rough rock scrambling—places where I can enjoy feeling challenged and

Have "Plan B" ready if your destination doesn't work

Roots like this on the trail offer dangerous tripping hazards, so take care when encountering these trail conditions

am able to take in my surroundings, while not feeling in danger of injuring myself with one misstep.

"Bog bridges" are elevated half-logs or two-by-twelve boards spanning boggy trail areas. Often these are too narrow or high to allow comfortable walking for me. Stopping to extend the length of my hiking poles so they reach the ground below, and then inching along what

Clear trail, few roots

feels like a tightrope is not much fun. Too much of this and I will turn around. Wider bog bridges would help, but require more labor and material costs and are unlikely to be available on the average hiking trail.

Success in navigating Easy Walks includes accepting that not every trail will be an Easy Walk. Have a Plan B ready if the chosen trail turns out to be unsuitable or becomes undesirable for continuing on.

Joni Mitchell sang years ago about the risks of "paving paradise." While I do not advocate paving all trails or making every trail accessible, it is exciting to find new Easy Walk locations!

Chapter 2
The Joys of Easy Walks

Easy Walks may not always offer the most spectacular scenery, or offer epic physical challenges. We who seek out Easy Walks often have other life challenges that preclude strenuous outings. For many years, I was unable to venture beyond the path (actually a quiet, paved, dead-end road) that took me alongside the lake near my home. These daily walks in every season offered me the opportunity not only to heal, but to closely study a small area.

During those years, life in the slow lane led me to a new appreciation of small things. Changing seasons brought migrating waterfowl, visiting otters, an osprey on the hunt, and thriving offspring of nesting swans each spring.

Stream peeking out from under the snow at Birchwold Farm, Wrentham, MA

Look for the small changes, the seasonal wonders, the surprises that occur quietly in the natural world all around us. By revisiting an area multiple times, you may learn to recognize the subtle changes so often missed by those intent only on exercise or socializing.

Life in the slow lane has benefits— Learn to embrace them

Spending time on a familiar trail in different seasons offers varied experiences and a broader appreciation of the landscape and wildlife. Edible plants and berries can turn an otherwise routine outing into a game of hide-and-seek as you search to find the next patch of tasty morsels. Please leave some for the next wanderer. When leaves are down, it is easier to see man-made changes to the surrounding landscape. Nests and wildlife trails are renewed and changed. Perennial plants return each year, offering beautiful colors not noticed in other seasons. Even the most familiar trail has the potential to surprise.

Canada geese on a local pond

Spring walks reveal the first signs of new growth, as well as young birds and animals just out of the nest, exploring quiet ponds. Migrating birds and waterfowl return and fill the woodlands and waterways with changing sights and sounds. Local rivers may be filled to the brim, or even overflowing. Low-lying trails may sometimes present muddy quagmires that are best avoided.

Summer and early fall often offer comfortable temperatures. Edible plants and berries enhance the experience. Avoid anything growing along power lines, which are often sprayed heavily with long-lasting pesticides.

Familiar trails can still surprise

Fall has glories all its own in New England and other northern climates, when the woods are ablaze with color. Migrating birds that paused the previous spring on their way north will be heading back south in the fall.

Ripening raspberries along a rail trail

Fresh snow in northern climates offers a wonderful opportunity to get outside. We sometimes spot animal tracks as tiny mice feet traverse the snow, and tunnels created by mice and voles burrowing underneath the snow. If we are lucky we might spot broad disturbances on the snow's surface where a hawk swept up its prey. Deer and coyote tracks abound in our area. Beavers and otters climb up and slide back down stream banks, leaving a worn path next to the water. Turkey footprints are everywhere. In a deep freeze, we can venture out to stream and shoreline areas not accessible the rest of the year. Fascinating patterns appear in the snow, ice, and sky. With the leaves down, we can observe varieties of land use and differing vegetative growth not apparent at other times of the year.

Winter walks in areas that offer no snow provide the

Nesting mute swan at a local pond

chance to experience the changes of season with new views of the landscape. These changes may be subtler, so repeated visits may be needed to pick up on these smaller changes. Learning to enjoy the subtleties of the landscape where you live adds dimension and enjoyment to familiar local walks.

Chapter 3
Where can we find Easy Walks?

Many of us long to escape the beaten track, to be in a more natural environment featuring woods, water, large boulders, or open fields. Consider these options:

- Established "walking trails" systems

- Rail trails

- Local, state, and national parks and town forests, including outdoor and historic properties

- Old woodland roads

- Jeep trails and old mining roads

- Federal and local flood control dams and dikes

- Historical sites and ruins

- Arboretums and nature centers

- Paths alongside rivers and streams

- Town commons

- Cemeteries, if open to the public

- Urban nature opportunities

- "Pick-your-own" farms

- Mountain views

- Established hiking trails

- Highway stops

- To discover trails, study maps, both topographic and local

- Investigate online maps and Google Earth.

Established "walking trail" systems

Talk with local friends, dog walkers, and others who frequent the outdoors to discover local trail systems that may not be well marked in your area. Many of these trails will be noted in online reviews, blog posts, and other sources that can provide you with basic information about where trails may be, along with their relative difficulty.

Rail trails

The U.S. interstate highway system eventually made thousands of miles of rail lines throughout the country obsolete. Visionaries realized that these abandoned rail corridors could be transformed into a network of walking

A former railroad line, now a rail trail, crosses Lake Champlain in Vermont, with views of the lake and mountains.
(South Hero Island, VT)

and biking trails. The work to accomplish this dream is ongoing, and has gained steam in the past decade.

Many rail trails presently have only one or a few short completed sections. Over time some have become linked into attractive multi-mile systems, allowing visitors to explore on foot or bicycle for hours or in some cases, for days. Unimproved former rail beds are rarely easily passable on bicycles, yet some stretches of proposed rail trail are manageable and attractive for bike riding once the ties have been removed.

We walk and ride on local dirt trails, as well as paved trails. We have had the joy of bicycling on our adaptive tandem for miles through a roadless river canyon on a rail trail in Pennsylvania. Granted, on that day-long trip we took breaks, and yes, some parts of us were more sore than others at the end of the day.

Every improved rail trail we have found offers an Easy Walk and a combination of natural and historic features of interest. Railroad rights-of-way have minimal slope and often cut right through waterways, offering open views of interesting ponds, swamps, rivers, and the wildlife within. In New England, many feature impressive hand-cut stone work at drainage culverts, bridges, and retaining walls. Interpretive signage and stops abound on many trails. Fascinating timber or steel bridges of historic construction may be next to or incorporated into the rail trail right-of-way. Often we find side paths and additional trail links off a rail trail.

Streams and swamps along the route break up any monotony that might arise from traversing a straight line through second-growth forest. These paths often allow views of heron rookeries, beaver activity, and other features not easily found in the normal course of a walk elsewhere.

Multiple state parks line the northern California coast, with expansive views of coastal headlands and rock formations off shore.

Local, state and national parks

Every state has lands set aside as parks, many with extensive trail systems. Our National Park system promotes creation

Yellowstone National Park boardwalks offer Easy Walks through otherwise challenging landscape.

of accessible trails within park confines. Provincial Parks we have visited in Canada offer accessible trails. Generally of short extent, these trails lead to popular highlights and feature graded pathways that are well-marked and maintained, and handicapped railings.

The existence of trails in a park does not guarantee that all or even some of the trails will be Easy Walks, but asking questions about the trails is a good place to start. We have spent time in various states exploring these wonderful open spaces, some of which offer Easy Walks to coastlines, views, or simple woodland trails.

Old farm roads in town forests and other publicly owned properties

The New England woods are full of old farm tracks and abandoned roads. They might not have been graded in a hundred years, yet someone once cleared the trees and removed most rocks—a vast improvement over bushwhacking through the forest. Some roads may not

Today's broad trails through woodlands were often well-traveled cart paths in years past. (Noon Hill, Medfield, MA)

be well maintained, while others have become part of established hiking trails. You may suddenly realize the trail you are on has widened considerably. When in the New York and New England regions, you may find stone walls lining both sides of this wider trail. These are sure signs that your woodland path was at some time a more heavily traveled (unpaved) cart path.

People created these cart tracks where they did for a reason. The route was generally the easier way to get from one point to another. Even today, they may be relatively accessible, if not flooded or simply too ingrown with vegetation. Be aware that these old paths may cross private property and easements may have been granted. Respect private property restrictions.

Stone walls in the U.S. are not generally as old as some might think. The majority were built beginning in the early 1800s in the United States, as the supply of local wood for fencing was depleted. The present day dry-laid (lacking mortar) stone walls we see in the woods were constructed in open pasture and surrounding cultivated land, marking boundaries and acting as a repository of unwanted stones. As farms in the east were abandoned in favor of more fertile land westward, trees and shrubs took root in these fields, creating what now are mature forests—and creating the illusion that the stone walls we see today were constructed in dense woodland.

Jeep trails and old mining roads

In the western U.S., jeep trails and old mining roads are ubiquitous and can offer a traceable trail through otherwise wild country. Accessibility varies. A walk across a sandstone cap-rock plain—that is, smooth bedrock—may offer a near-pavement experience. A climb up steep hillsides or slopes of loose rock talus is unlikely to be desirable or an Easy Walk.

Dam and flood control sites that are open to the public

Flood control structures (dams, dikes) when publicly accessible often offer Easy Walks. These water features are flat by their nature. Interesting historical, manmade, and natural features abound. Please note that many drinking water reservoirs are not open to the public.

Flood control structures often create open areas well suited for enjoying Easy Walks. (West Hill Dam, Uxbridge, MA)

Historical sites/ruins

Historical sites and/or ruins may offer Easy Walks simply because they have been used over the centuries by people who have accessed them and even beaten down the paths to get to them. They may be overseen by nonprofit or public agencies that offer maps or guided tours. Inquire about trail conditions.

Nature Centers and Arboretums

Parklands and nature centers with trails owned by Audubon societies, Trustees of Reservations, the Nature Conservancy, various land trusts, and other nonprofits often have well-managed trail systems built with

Well-traveled paths led to these pictures inscribed in stone, Arizona.

accessibility in mind. Many have online listings and/or printed guidebooks.

Arboretums are designed with Easy Walk walking paths and offer sun and shade and careful labels that help put names to native plants. When traveling far afield, we have found they provide a helpful introduction to a new area and its habitats. Some local libraries lend out arboretum passes. Inquire locally.

We enjoy exploring a local arboretum near us in Acton, Massachusetts, which offers varied landscapes, from broad open meadows to muddy swamps. A garden features a wealth of herbs and plants common throughout the growing season. Flowers fill the walkways. The swamp has a boardwalk that offers views of the water and plants below.

An arboretum in Tucson, Arizona, gave us the opportunity to not only enjoy native plants, but also to see birds native to that area that were totally new to us.

Walkways, benches, and shade are often featured at local arboretums. (Acton, MA)

Encountering native birds challenged us to learn how to better use our bird guides in the hopes of identifying them. By the end of our visit, besides having grown to recognize many new (to us) plants, we welcomed these strange birds that had become familiar, a delight to see each time one appeared.

Paths along rivers, streams, and ponds

Historically, towns and industry grew up around water travel and water power. Old roads abound near formerly developed ponds and rivers with dams and diversion structures. In the dry American West, many water features were manmade and therefore required access roads. Rivers everywhere offered a traceable navigation route through otherwise confusing and varied topography, and frequently featured old, sometimes abandoned, roads on one or both sides.

In becoming familiar with maps, you will learn to discern where waterways are, as well as how to locate various open-space properties. In years past, rivers and streams were regarded as convenient sewer systems. People turned their backs on these waterways and used them as convenient dumping grounds for trash of all kinds. Structures were built over rivers and streams, the water was funneled through culverts, and some entire river systems were even paved over! People did almost anything to get away from what our industrial revolution had fouled.

Trails near waterways tend to be flatter, are not as likely to be rocky, and often have water views

In the 1970s, the first "Earth Day" was announced, and since this time, important national clean-water and clean-air legislation has been enacted. Rivers, such as the Cuyahoga River near Cleveland, Ohio, were once so polluted they caught on fire (it was actually the oil slick on the Cuyahoga that burned in 1969, while two bridges were destroyed). Since then, with the help of an army of citizen volunteers, and with the cooperation of local, state and national governments, many rivers, including the Cuyahoga, have been cleaned up and restored to a level that is clean enough to provide welcome places for recreation and respite.

Rather than places to avoid, these riverfront landscapes have become magnets for the development of trails, parks, and other passive forms of outdoor recreation. Some of the most popular rail trails we travel on near our home offer views of local rivers that were once highly polluted. Additional trails, both formal walking trails and trails created by local fisherfolk, provide pathways along the banks of local streams and ponds.

When looking for Easy Walks, keep in mind that trails near waterways are often flatter, are not as likely to be rocky, and often offer water views from the trail as well. The canal building craze of the early 1800s in the eastern U.S. created flat tow paths for horses or mules to traverse as they hauled goods on barges through these canals. Most canals were later abandoned or destroyed by massive floods, and were nearly forgotten as more dependable railroad networks took over the job of transporting goods from where they were produced to markets eager for these products. The building of these canals, with their necessary tow paths, created a network of potential trails, some of which have been restored, while others are in the process of being restored and turned into improved pathways. Because they were built alongside waterways, these tow paths offer both water views and historical insight into environmental, economic, and political forces that led to their creation and later abandonment.

Look for trails around lakes and ponds. Usually some of the trail will be rough, rooty, or swampy. It is a rare treat to find an Easy Walk all the way around a water body, and almost always is the result of intentional planning by the trail builder to overcome drainage challenges.

Rivers may have trails that follow the path of the waterway, sometimes on both sides. Some ocean beaches

Restored tow path, along of the Blackstone Canal. The bridge in this picture would not have been present when the canal was in operation. (Uxbridge, MA)

have marshes nearby, which may have boardwalks, manmade dikes, or other pathways created to facilitate access to the area.

Other places to find Easy Walks:

Town commons, greens, and town parks

Town commons or village greens may offer walking paths, benches, shade trees, and perhaps even a gazebo for community events in these public spaces. Local groups may have weekly walking events that utilize a local town common or public park, offering social opportunities as well as gentle exercise. Check with local senior or community centers to learn whether they sponsor a walking group at your local town common. YMCAs also sponsor walking groups, usually with little or no charge for participation.

Many communities have common areas, or public greens, with paved walkways, benches, historical markers and monuments to add interest to your visit.(Bellingham, MA)

On visits to local cemeteries, bring your appreciation of local history and those who lived before. (Mendon, MA)

Cemeteries

Cemeteries feature walkable paths by design. Large trees provide welcome shade; birds may frequent the area. The residents are certainly quiet, and no power lines will obstruct your views. Before starting your walk, do your homework to confirm that visitors are allowed, respect hours the cemetery is open, and obey parking restrictions. A call to the local town hall is a good place to start to obtain information on visiting local cemeteries, in the absence of posted signs at the cemeteries themselves.

In the early 1800s some cemeteries were designed specifically as garden cemeteries, as opposed to the church graveyards that were common in cities prior to this time. Mt. Auburn in Cambridge, Massachusetts, the first garden cemetery in the U.S., offers bird-watching opportunities and interpretative walks. These cemeteries declined in popularity later in the 19th century as they fell into disrepair and true public parks were constructed. Most of the remaining garden cemeteries are now run by nonprofits.

Urban nature opportunities

Various cities have organizations that offer walking tours featuring historical points of interest that make each city distinctive. Boston By Foot offers walking tours to various parts of the city, and private tours can be arranged, while Boston's famous Freedom Trail features a brick walkway within the city's sidewalks that you can follow to points of historical interest throughout the city.

Beware uneven paving stones and walkways in older U.S. cities

In Massachusetts, Mass Audubon has nature centers situated in Boston and Worcester that offer nature programs specifically aimed at encouraging urban children, youth, and families to enjoy the outdoors. Local zoos and urban parks also offer green space for city dwellers hungry to enjoy green growing things.

Urban areas offer multiple options for Easy Walks, with surprising opportunities for family fun. (Boston Public Gardens' renowned Make Way for Ducklings statues).

Pick-your-own farms

Getting outdoors to pick your own fruit, flowers, or other crops is a great opportunity to spend time outside and come home with fresh food to share with your family. However, most farms and orchards are not created with walkers in mind. Paths between trees and bushes are designed for mowers to access to keep grass and weeds down. Groundhogs may dig holes in fields. Please respect

Picking your own fruit is a wonderful part of summer, whether from your own yard or a local farm.

designated pathways. When at your local pick-your-own farm, never push through plantings or walk in undesignated areas.

Never eat fruit from along utility lines—The areas are heavily sprayed with chemicals

Farms are sunny by their nature. Be sure to use sunblock and wear sun hats. Wearing light-colored clothing will make easier the necessary tick checks that should follow at the end of the day. We have found that pesticide residues from spraying can linger and affect those susceptible to rashes or asthma. Wash yourself and all fruits thoroughly before consuming or freezing. (Warning: Never consume fruits found along utility lines, since they are usually heavily aerially sprayed with the strongest of chemicals.)

In season one can pick many pounds of fruit fairly quickly. Reward yourself by trying this favorite recipe of ours:

Rewards for taking Easy Walks come in many forms, like this easy berry pie.

Fresh Berry Pie

Ingredients

One approximately nine-inch-diameter pie shell, baked until firm

Five cups fresh blueberries, strawberries, or other fruit, washed, leaves and stems removed

Two teaspoons lemon juice

One cup sugar (I tend to reduce to ¾ cup)

Three tablespoons cornstarch

Directions

1. Take about three cups of berries and mash or blend them roughly in a pot. Stir in lemon juice, cornstarch, and sugar. Cook over medium heat until thickened, stirring constantly. Cool slightly.

2. Spread remaining fresh, uncrushed and washed berries in bottom of baked pie shell, then pour cooked berry "pudding" over fresh berries.

3. Chill a few hours until set. Eat as is, or serve with whipped cream or ice cream.

Mountain views

There is something wonderful about a view and taking the time to enjoy the sight of the landscape stretching out into the distance. Many of these views are the reward for those capable of arduous hikes up difficult paths.

Some mountains have roads leading to summits— Enjoy the views

It is a rare and special opportunity to find a mountain with an access road one can drive up. Whether to a local hilltop

A road can facilitate visits on foot or by car to the top of some mountains. (Mt. Holyoke, Hadley, MA)

or a spectacularly high mountain, public access roads make it easy to enjoy views while gaining a better understanding of an area. When possible on mountain roads, we like to make stops on the way up and down, to explore side paths and viewpoints. Ski areas may allow free or paid access to certain roads, off-season.

Hiking Trails

If you never get out, you'll never know what's there

Many "hiking trails" may be accessible for at least a portion of their length. The challenge is to scope them out ahead of time to avoid long travel for a short visit. Scoping may be done by a willing spouse or friend, via online communication, consultation with trail owners and maintainers, or by consulting other venues.

While driving

When driving on country roads, stop to get out of the car to investigate features. That pull-off by the road may lead to a trailhead, waterfall, mountain view, pond walk, historical site, or another interesting feature. If you never get out of your car, you will never know what was there.

Chapter 4:
Tools and Strategies for
Finding Easy Walks

Here are some of the tools and strategies we use when searching out new places to get outdoors:

- Learn to read maps.

- The internet has multiple resources to help find trails and reviews of trails.

- Google Earth is a great tool for investigating an area before traveling.

- Visitors bureaus in tourist destinations can point you in the right direction.

- Search social networks, like Facebook, Instagram, and others, to ask for help locating trails in specific areas.

- Senior centers and community centers often have local walking groups with knowledgeable leaders.

- Word of mouth—tell people you are looking for Easy Walks.

- Written publications offer great details about specific areas.

- Time visits to avoid crowds.

- With care, get out and explore!

Maps

Many online maps use the U.S.G.S. (U.S. Geological Survey) as a base and will show trails as a single dotted line

Visually impaired friends investigate carved wooden map at Oak Grove Farm, Millis, MA.

and old roads as a double dotted line. Whenever we see these lines we know to investigate online or in person to see if an Easy Walk is in the area.

Map reading is not difficult. The unpracticed may need help at first to relate the scale marker to map distances, translate contour lines into an understanding of slope or flatness, or pick out the trail, parking, or water features. A map may not show you the big picture of where a trail is or how to get there. The map may be of such large scale (less detail) that you really can't tell much about the actual trail. We often couple the use of a trail map with a road atlas or online GPS map to locate a trail. Maps that exhibit U.S.G.S. conventions, with scale, north arrow, elevation contours, and clearly differentiated trails and abandoned roads are preferable to "cartoon" maps, that is, hand drawn maps of variable accuracy and scale.

While most of us have forgotten or never learned to use a compass, cell phones with GPS apps are ubiquitous. Learn to read a map and identify general compass direction. Is your car parked in that direction, or directly opposite? You better be able to tell! And while cell phone coverage has greatly improved in the past several years in many areas, be aware that especially in more hilly and mountainous areas, cell phone coverage is not dependable.

We have found some of our favorite spots for Easy Walks by simply looking at maps to see what is in the vicinity of our planned travels. Dotted lines and apparent old roads on maps are worthy of further investigation.

Keep in mind when reading maps that you can discover a tremendous amount of information once you understand a few basic mapping principles:

1. Widely spaced contour lines show more level ground, tightly spaced lines show the ground is quite steep.

2. Swampy areas are marked by grass-tuft-like symbols.

3. Areas near swamps, or with high groundwater nearby at about the same elevation, may have trails with lots of roots. Trees cannot breathe underwater, so if the groundwater is quite high in an area, tree roots will stay close to the surface, presenting tripping hazards.

Over time, you may become familiar with the different terrains and geology of your area. Glacial outwash plains (often found near waterways) feature sandy soils and walkable trails, where not flooded. Hilly, rocky terrain may look intriguing, but often has intensely rocky trails. Wet, non-draining soils may offer muddy trails, or produce trails with a tricky tangle of shallow tree roots.

One deep forest trail is soft and loamy; another impenetrably rocky and rooty. It's fun to think about and seek out information to help understand the differences. Local nature guides may provide a better understanding of how geology and glacial history in your area created the terrain.

While it is difficult to discern the width of a trail from reading a map, you may see indications that a trail is "improved." We often look on Google Earth in these cases to see if we can gain any more information about the condition of a trail before we head out.

Internet searches

Often the obvious place to start your search for local Easy Walks is online. Without appropriate search terms however, the results can be unexpected or overwhelming. Many trail websites are created by volunteers, and the accuracy of information is spotty. Websites may be out of date.

Specific cellphone apps. such as TrailLink, offer a plethora of locale-specific trails, but less often offer much information regarding trail conditions or accessibility. Most of TrailLink's maps appear to be self-generated by users' GPS tracking, offering a sometimes overlapping and confusing appearance.

We prefer to look for useful site descriptions, parking information, and trail maps that are often put online by owner/manager organizations. These include Audubon Societies, Trustees of Reservations, Nature Conservancy, Army Corps of Engineers, local/state/national parks, historical societies, watershed management organizations, and others. Many towns maintain a listing of their managed Open Spaces. Look under Conservation Commission on town websites.

Sometimes owner/manager agencies intentionally withhold information in order to limit usage to manageable levels. If you know of a managed trail yet cannot find it online, a phone call to the local town hall or an online inquiry may elicit more information.

An app we have enjoyed using while on the trail is called Rockd (www.rockd.org). It brings up the geological map of the area you are in. We often find that the local geology controls the topography. After consulting this app, we often can recognize that nearby water and road features align with changes in bedrock type or fault zones. Stark differences in vegetation can be due to changes in bedrock and overlying soils.

Google Earth

Google Earth is a great online resource and aid to trip planning. We have used this website/app to research the location and condition of rail trails in a great many locations.

A printed description or contour map may not tell us how interesting a trail is. For example, water features often add interest to an outing. Looking at Google Earth often allows us to see the route, the possible water features, and sometimes to discern whether a path appears improved or unimproved. We have been able to spot ponds, follow rivers and streams, and see how the trail intersects with these waterways, so we can make more informed decisions about where we want to visit. Google Earth has also been a great tool helping me prepare accurate maps used in my Easy Walks book series.

Visitors' bureaus

When spending time in tourist destination areas, visitors' bureaus are great places to pick up maps, tide charts, calendars of local events during your visit, and to meet people who often live nearby year-round. These staff people are great resources for obtaining helpful information about where you might be able to find Easy Walks.

Park rangers and visitor centers are the best resources to answer the question, "Where can I go that everyone else isn't?" Often they are tasked with spreading out visitation and will be delighted to spend a few minutes advising you.

Take your time, ask a few questions, then express your appreciation for the area you are in. Note that you are looking for Easy Walks, being specific about what you are interested in. You may learn of hidden gems that are not well publicized.

Online social networks

I have made some dear friends who I first encountered through local hiking groups on Facebook. My Facebook book page, *Easy Walks in Massachusetts*, helps publicize my series of walking books. I have also run a Facebook group for several years, Easy Walks, Massachusetts, RI and Nearby. On this forum group members are invited to share places to go, local events, educational information, and volunteer opportunities. These include meet-ups for group walks, trail clean-ups, outdoor education events, and trail closures.

Use common sense in online postings— Keep your personal information private

Facebook, Instagram, and Meetup, to name a few social networks now available, have multiple groups that often have a geographic focus. These social network platforms have search mechanisms that allow you to look for others in your geographic area who have similar interests, compatible physical abilities or disabilities. Hike it, Baby! is a group that helps families with young ones meet to walk together at set times and places. Both Facebook and Instagram have groups that focus on those with disabilities, as well as those who have been otherwise marginalized because of body size, sexual orientation, ethnic type, or skin color. These groups offer inspiration, group events, and education to provide encouragement to get outside and be more active.

Please remember that anything you post online could be permanent. Use common sense in online postings or discussions, and keep your personal information private.

Local senior centers and community centers

Local senior centers, adult education organizations, and community centers often have weekly walking groups. If not in your specific town, perhaps a nearby town will have them. Easiest way to find out? Check their websites, of course! Or give them a call. They may walk on site, or travel to favorite local walking spots. Regardless, this is a great resource for meeting other local walkers and getting information about the local area.

Word of mouth

Simply bringing up the topic of walking when meeting people in new places has revealed to us hidden gems in communities we were not familiar with. Letting folks know you are looking for local places to walk will often result in near-strangers suddenly compiling lists of places you really must visit. You may learn of existing local walking groups you could join, usually for little or no cost. You may also hear more than you bargained for about nearby and far-flung places that others have visited!

> **Not every outing will be an Easy Walk**

Just because you have listened to someone's recommendations does not mean these suggestions are great places for you to find Easy Walks. You are the best judge of whether any particular outdoor location will work well with your individual life challenges.

Publications

An amazing variety of magazines, online articles, and lists of "best of" places, many with color photos, are published with the intent of inviting the reader to get outdoors. What is sometimes missing from these articles is the bigger picture of how to prepare, how hard it might be to find an exact location, where to park, whether there is an entrance fee, the best time of year to visit, and more.

To learn more, look up websites to find more information about trails you read about. Try sending an email to the author to ask more specific questions. You may receive further recommendations. Often the word limit in these articles prevents the author from including details you need to know if you really want to explore.

Be willing to explore

Sometimes photos don't do justice to an area. It may turn out to be more beautiful than any photograph could show. Other times, just beyond the photo is an unsightly dump, a super highway, or something else that detracts from the experience.

Keep a file of "Bucket list" destinations, so when the opportunity arises, you'll have a choice of places available to explore, rather than resorting only to the same places visited many times in the past. Not every outing will turn out to be an Easy Walk. It's all part of the adventure.

Explore!

Often when we drive somewhere my husband has slowed, found a safe place to turn around, and pulled off to investigate an interesting trailhead or feature just spotted. We may decide the area is worth taking a few minutes to check out, for future visitation. Other times, the area looks so challenging that we head on our way, knowing we will come across other more accessible places to visit in the future. I have learned to simply wait a few minutes when these sudden about-faces occur, since all will soon be revealed.

This happened recently when we were traveling through New Jersey enroute to a distant conference. My husband did a quick U-turn and we headed back in the opposite direction. He had spotted a sign: "Lizard Tail Swamp Preserve." While amusement with the name is what caught his eye, we found a welcome break from driving plus an Easy Walk through a unique ecological zone of holly bush and woodlands.

Avoid crowds—pay attention to timing

Visits to popular parks and other outdoor areas may not be Easy Walks due to crowding. Our preference is to enjoy the trail so we can take in our surroundings rather than having

You never know what might await when you see signs like "Lizard Tail Swamp Preserve." (Cape May, NJ)

to pay close attention to other people. Due to my balance issues, the presence of crowds creates a safety concern. For those who don't wish to visit the trail along with "a thousand of your closest friends," here are a few strategies we use to try to avoid crowded trails:

- During popular weekends, stay away from "greatest hits" trails to explore something less used. The views may be less spectacular. The experience, however, will be more enjoyable.

- Pick less popular weekdays and early morning hours. We try to visit the more popular national parks off-season when possible.

- Head out when skies are overcast. Many wait to hit the trail on sunny days. (Be sure to bring along your rain gear.)

- If you've traveled far, it may be worth viewing those "greatest hits" locations. However, try to visit in the early morning hours, or around suppertime, when fewer people are on the trail.

- We like to carry with us a simple picnic lunch or snacks, giving us the option to stay out and explore longer within our own timeframe. When touring the national parks, we usually find fewer folks on those trails near roads when it is closer to mealtimes.

Chapter 5
Equipment for Easy Walks

We make it a habit to throw certain items in a daypack, no matter how short a planned outing. These items vary with the season and the terrain. Being prepared has often allowed us to travel farther and stay outside longer. Of course, a casual stroll in your own neighborhood may require few of the items we detail in this chapter. Here is a list of items we use at various times of the year and under differing weather conditions:

- Sturdy footgear with a good grip

- Layers of clothing

- Extra clothing packed for ease of access—conditions do change

- Sunhat, sunscreen, insect repellent

- Rain jacket and rain pants when needed

- Appropriate winter gear: insulated boots with good grip; hats and gloves; layered clothing; face protection

- Daypack

- Headlamp

- Hiking poles

- Water bottle, snacks, and bag for trash

- When accompanying those with special needs of any kind (including age-related, mobility challenges, or children), bring extra of anything you might already have thought of.

Bring extra
Think ahead

Sturdy footwear

Sandals or flip flops are never a good choice on the trail. If you walk frequently, a good pair of lightweight hiking boots will give you more support, stability, and flexibility than sneakers or walking shoes. Vibram brand or equivalent "lug sole" soles are like snow tires on your car. You can negotiate the occasional icy, rocky, or muddy patch far better with this type of footwear. Thorns and rocks can quickly puncture thin soles. We have seen the soles of cheap shoes tear completely off during a skid or slip.

Break in your new boots at home. Otherwise, you will be sure to generate blisters while you are on the trail. Socks that have lost their elastic tend to bunch up or slide down right off your feet inside your boots. We avoid putting hiking socks in the dryer, since heat damages the elastic.

In icy conditions, some people swear by using Yaktrax®, or other brands of removable strap-on winter traction gear to maintain safer footing on icy trails. Since these change both gait and balance I cannot use them. Hard ice is hard, no matter the footwear. Some conditions are best avoided.

Hard ice is hard, no matter the footwear

Layers: the key to preparedness

Temperatures can swing dramatically as the sun comes up or sets, or as one approaches windy ocean or mountaintop areas. After you get out of your car and before embarking on a longer walk, ask yourself:

- In cool weather: If I'm comfortable just standing around, am I prepared to shed layers later as I warm up? When it gets colder or windier, will I be cold? Instead of a heavyweight winter jacket, two or three layers offer more flexibility. In winter, however, we still pack our heaviest down jackets as backup in case we must stop for an extended time.

> **No jacket will keep you warm if your skin is moist or your feet are wet**

- In warm weather: If I'm comfortable now, will I be too warm later and need to shed layers? Instead of a single stadium jacket, wearing a light T-shirt, overshirt, polypropylene jacket or sweater, and a breathable rain jacket will offer flexibility for changing conditions during the day.

- In the unlikely event I am delayed on the trail for many hours (lost, injured, tired, or just can't bear to leave when planned) do I have appropriate clothing for a forty-degree temperature change later?

- Sweat and moisture are the enemy of staying warm. No jacket will keep you warm if your skin is moist or your feet are wet. Winter hikes, rainy days, and seashore visits are when we carry an extra T-shirt and pair of socks to change into if needed.

> **Wise clothing purchases are an investment**

Hats and sunscreen, insect repellent

Hats are an important accessory, summer or winter, for sun or frostbite protection. Summer hats with chinstraps stay on much better in windy conditions. We have several winter hats of varying thicknesses to suit conditions. Stocking hats, hats with ear coverings, or thick hats of multiple layers are all options for winter weather. It may take some time to find the hat or hats that work best for you.

Sunscreen should be reapplied throughout the day when spending extended (more than two hours) time outdoors. Face, neck, arms, and legs (front and back of legs, especially if you are biking or paddling) should all be covered with sunscreen to prevent both burns and the additional damage that extended time in the sun can cause.

Insect repellent is often necessary, especially if mosquitos are present. Ticks are a problem year-round. While insect repellents may help ward these critters off, keeping pants tucked into socks, avoiding bushwhacking through woods, and staying on cleared trails, are tick avoidance strategies. Tick checks are still important to do routinely after spending time in the outdoors, whether you choose to use insect repellent or not.

Prepare for the unexpected

Chiggers are an issue in more southern areas. Avoid them by staying out of brushy areas and not lying directly on the ground.

Rain gear

Over the years we have found that cheaper rain gear does not breathe, making you sweaty and uncomfortable. Ponchos blow around, performing poorly when on the trail. Rain jackets are much preferred. Waterproofing coatings wear off and leave you soaked when you most need protection. Not all expensive "breathable" fabrics are equal.

After buying numerous disappointing styles of rain gear over the years, we finally spent the money for real Gore-Tex® jackets. (It would have been cheaper to do so initially.) While we always carry our Gore-Tex® uninsulated jackets, we only bring rain pants if we plan on being out in the rain for a while or for needed wind protection on cold, windy days.

Winter gear

Hiking boots will not keep your feet warm in cold weather. We use Sorel® insulated hiking boots in winter. They have lug-type soles to provide sound footing in somewhat slippery conditions.

> **Mittens keep fingers warmer than isolating each finger with gloves**

Mittens are more effective at keeping fingers warm than isolating each finger with gloves. My mittens are either double knit, or insulated leather-type mittens that will not wear through as quickly as other mittens, since I put more stress on my mittens by always using hiking poles when walking on trails.

Layered clothing was referred to earlier in this chapter, an important "tool" to use in colder weather. Face protection is essential in the coldest weather. We use pullover knit face coverings that allow for ease of breathing, with room to safely see our surroundings as well.

Daypacks

A daypack provides a place to store needed gear for use along the trail. Extra layers of clothing can be carried in this pack, or use it to stash layers as they are removed. A pack of this type also allows for carrying water bottles, snacks, and any emergency equipment or medicine that might be needed.

Headlamps

Headlamps keep hands free and allow for focus on what is ahead. If we start out in the afternoon, we bring headlamps after testing to be sure the batteries are still good. Light in weight, they could make all the difference if we are delayed

Hiking poles can make all the difference in accessing places that are otherwise too unstable or rocky to visit safely.

on the trail beyond our plans. On a short walk we can linger and enjoy a beautiful sunset, knowing we have this safety gear to aid our return. Be aware that trails can look quite different at dusk and dark; wayfinding can become an unplanned challenge.

Hiking poles

Hiking poles are now commonplace aids for trail walkers, offering stability and balance and reducing stress on

> **Hiking poles help maintain balance on uneven trails**

worn-out knees. Adding readily available rubber tips to the metal ends quiets them on rock and reduces their tendency to skid. We use three-piece adjustable poles which can be disassembled to fit into a suitcase or pack. Using a pair, rather than a single pole, enhances stability and is less likely to result in arm strain. Garden gloves can be helpful hand protection on a pole-assisted long walk. Hiking poles not only support balance but can also serve as a warning to others to avoid careless behavior or crowding the user when traveling on trails, in cities, and in airports.

Other items to bring:

- Glasses and medications as necessary

- Printed map (What will you do if your cellphone drops or fails?)

- Snacks. Whether walking with adults or small children, packing water bottles and baggies of gorp, fruit, or energy bars can make the difference between continuing your outing and being compelled to make an early return trip. Bring an extra plastic bag to carry out your trash. Please, never leave orange peels or the like on or off the trail. It ruins the view for others and can encourage skunks and other nuisance animals.

Preparedness for participants with disabilities

Those with a disability or physical challenges of any type (advanced age, excess weight, pregnancy, stroller, or other mobility issues) especially need a little extra planning for changing outdoor conditions. If you cannot simply dash back up the trail when conditions change, be fully prepared. If escorting someone in this category, you have a broader responsibility to ensure that they remain safe and relatively comfortable no matter what transpires on your walk. Carry a larger pack and extra gear for them.

Chapter 6
Outdoor Safety on Easy Walks

Weather, temperature changes, and trail conditions will bring surprises to many out on trails. We are often met by other wet, cold, or weary hikers who say, "I wish I'd thought of that," while pointing to our coats, hats, or hiking poles. This chapter focuses on preparedness. We offer it as an educational guide and checklist.

While there is much to love about the outdoors, it comes with risk: weather, poison ivy, sunburn, ticks and other hazards. Preparedness leaves us more comfortable and ready to enjoy another day outdoors.

- Check temperature range predictions and prepare accordingly.

- Check weather and fire-risk reports in advance.

- Anticipate high water or flood conditions after storm events.

- Anticipate seasonal trail surface changes—snow, ice, slippery leaves, and acorns.

- Bring extra clothes on winter outings.

- Leave substantial extra time for stops to assure getting back before dark.

- Learn to recognize poison ivy and its cousins.

- Prepare to encounter mosquitos, ticks, chiggers, or other insects.

- Check tide charts before heading to the shore.

- Beautiful views often combine with steep drop-offs. Be cautious.

- Blaze-orange clothing is essential during hunting seasons.

Temperature

Temperatures can fluctuate forty or more degrees in the course of a walk, with rising or setting sun, weather fronts, and rising or falling winds. Mountaintop, desert, and shoreline areas are especially volatile. Wind and moisture drastically alter the difference between actual and "real-feel" temperature. Be prepared with suitable clothing layers.

Yesterday's rain can turn today's walk into a challenge

Water may be your only effective means of cooling down someone who becomes overheated. Carry extra water and manage your reserve for this purpose in hot weather. We have found an eight-ounce plastic spray mister filled with water to be indispensable for cooling, and refill it from our water bottle in the course of a walk. Some people are unable to sweat, others are prone to overheating. Carry a spray mister when accompanying them.

Weather

With cell phones, it is easy to keep track of local weather. Adapt the length, location, or type of outing to ensure a safe return from the outdoors well before any weather events. Avoid high rocky areas when there is risk of lightning. A common error is trying to complete a walk or achieve a peak or view in the face of oncoming weather. Turn around; this destination will be there for another day.

Fire risk is a serious concern in parts of the country. Be aware of fire-risk conditions and choose your outing carefully.

Be aware of wind chill, pay attention to weather reports, and avoid woods on extremely windy days, when branches may fall. In colder weather it is important to avoid sweating, which could soak clothes. Be prepared for stops when you need more clothing.

High water

Flash flooding, high water, flooded trails, and slippery conditions can result from high rain or snowmelt conditions. While we often look ahead to tomorrow's weather forecasts, it is helpful to be mindful of recent weather as well, understanding that yesterday's rain may make today's walk more challenging. Local rivers can flood their banks, producing unpredictable trail conditions near these rivers. Eroded trails readily become waterways during heavy runoff events.

Seasonal challenges

Slippery leaves, rolling acorns, ice and snow, mud, and puddles are all seasonal challenges. Winter snows can quickly become crusty and icy on trails that have been walked on, as they thaw and refreeze repeatedly. Too often we travel to a trailhead only to find the trail an icy slick despite walkable snow beside it. In such circumstances, we turn around or look for an untracked area for a shorter walk.

We have ventured along a windy shoreline at extreme temperatures (-10 F) for several hours and been comfortable with suitable preparation, including face masks, layered socks in loose insulated boots, doubled mittens (not gloves), doubled hats and hoods, and careful layering of clothing. As the morning warmed up we had to peel off layers, only to throw everything back on when the wind picked up. It is critical to keep airspace around fingers and toes and not wear anything snug. Of course, with all this clothing on, you may not be able to easily get back up if you fall over! A good reason not to walk alone. Watching seabirds diving into the ocean in this weather certainly offers a bracing perspective on the concept of staying warm.

You can almost always return another day

Bring extra clothes with you

Dress in layers, protect your face, head, and hands, and be sure you have socks that will stay on your feet (worn-out elastic leads to socks slipping down into your boots.) As you warm up you may need to shed layers, only to need them later when resting or conditions change.

Daylight

Seasonal daylight fluctuations can take people by surprise. With the ubiquity of cell phones having weather apps, there is no excuse to be unaware of the timing of sunset these days.

Adjacent mountains often hide the setting sun several hours earlier than expected. Plan accordingly. Traveling

One example of poison ivy leaves

outside your normal region? Time-zones and latitude changes may catch you off guard.

For any significant outing, visit to an unfamiliar area, or walk after midday, it's good practice to carry a working headlamp in your pack or coat pocket. Intentional or unintentional delays can be better handled if you can see your way. If you or those you are with need special accommodations, it is important to allow for additional daylight time to

Poison ivy and ticks take the fun out of the best planned outing

Every part of the poison ivy plant is noxious—roots as well as leaves. A healthy poison ivy hairy root system climbs up a tree.

complete your outing. Don't have enough time? Shorten your walk or plan to come back another day.

Poisonous Plants

Poison ivy is ubiquitous throughout the eastern U.S., and poison oak is found in parts of the west. Become familiar with these plants and look for them at both trail level and overhead! Leaf color and shape can vary quite dramatically for poison ivy, often looking like something else. Vines climbing trees are distinctly hairy.

If exposed to poison ivy or its relatives, getting to a source of soap and water as soon as possible can prevent much future misery. The urushiol oil present in poison ivy and its cousins can remain active for months or even years on boots and clothing, and can cause second-hand rashes, as we have found to our chagrin. In shorts-wearing season, one of us re-discovers this yearly; squatting on one's heels allows an infected boot to create new rashes on the leg. The rest of the year seems to pass uneventfully. The Technu® brand is (an expensive) soap for washing clothing or gear to help remove urushiol oil. Alternatives have not worked well for us.

Insects

Mosquitos are ubiquitous in wet areas. Illnesses of various sorts are associated with mosquito bites, including West Nile virus and EEE virus. Many over-the-counter repellents are available; use what you are comfortable with. Some repellents will stain clothing. Alcohol-based wipes can be a useful accessory for hand-cleaning after applying repellent.

Ticks can be active throughout the year, even in colder months. Lyme disease and Rocky Mountain spotted fever are among the many serious illnesses passed on by different types of ticks. In tick-heavy areas wear light-colored pants to make ticks more visible, tuck pant legs into socks, and perform thorough tick checks after being outdoors. Taking a shower upon your return home also aids in washing off ticks you may have missed.

A lint remover is a handy tool to catch ticks you may not have seen on your clothing. Crush ticks before disposing. Tossing clothes into your dryer for twenty minutes after an outing may desiccate tiny ticks remaining on your clothing.

Chiggers are found in much of the South. In areas with chiggers, avoid tall grassy areas, and do not lie on the ground. Spanish moss is a favored habitat. If bitten by chiggers, over-the-counter treatments can treat the extreme itch produced by these critters (they are actually in the spider family). Painting nail polish on chigger bites is also effective in reducing the itch. The same tactics used to prevent ticks will help discourage chiggers: tucking pants into socks, wearing tightly-woven fabric clothing, and spraying clothing with insecticides containing DEET or permethrin.

Wasps, hornets, and bees are common in many outdoor environments. Venomous stings can not only be painful, but for those with allergies, stings can be dangerous, even life-threatening. If you have been prescribed an EpiPen® (injectable epinephrine), always carry it on walks. Be sure others know of your allergy and where to find your medication.

In some parts of the country, insect hazards include black widow or brown recluse spiders, scorpions, or fire ants. When traveling afar, learn about local hazards and what to look for. In western or southern areas look before sitting down, check boots before putting them on, and check under outhouse seats before using!

Tides

Tide charts for coastal areas are available in newspapers and many shops, as well as online. Checking on times for low or high tide before walking to or along the shore is important for safety, and can also tell you when you are more likely to see birds, seals, or other sea life that feed near shore. We have noticed that most often seabirds are closest to shore and more actively feeding at low tides.

Drop-offs

Views are often the best at the top of steep drop-offs. Watch smaller children, and older or off-balance adults to ensure they do not tumble off cliffs, and watch footing to avoid tripping near the edge of a drop-off.

Beautiful views often have sharp drop-offs. Beware.

Animal encounters

Animal hazards are unlikely to be an issue when on Easy Walks on the East Coast. Other parts of the country will have different levels of risk for animal encounters, so do your best to learn about the risks and how to prepare. Skunks or bears may frequent campgrounds and popular trail heads, looking for trash. Snakes sunning on a quiet trail are a chance to observe nature quietly. Encounters of these types are rare.

Encountering this wild moose and her calf was exciting, but also alarming because of the potential for the mother to become aggressive while protecting her calf. (Cape Breton, Nova Scotia)

Sharing the woods with hunters

We rarely encounter hunters on our walks. Many public properties restrict hunting. Others specifically share the land with hunters, so when walking in the fall, taking precautions is necessary.

Check your state's laws for hunting season dates—they change yearly. Just as the leaves begin to turn, hunters start venturing out into various public and private lands. Everyone out in the woods is strongly encouraged, while in some states are required, to wear as much blaze-orange as possible. An orange hat is not sufficient. Orange vests or orange jackets are recommended. Purchase orange vests that are large enough to fit over whatever layers of clothing you will need in variable fall temperatures.

> **An orange hat in hunting season is not sufficient!**

Clothing

Your choice of clothing can be an asset, a hindrance, or an outright hazard. My husband served with search and rescue teams for some years and encountered instances where falls and injuries resulted from loss of balance caused by loose gear.

Camera and water bottle straps often catch branches, and equipment can toss about while walking. They can throw a person off-balance. Best to store items on a proper harness or in a pack.

Double knot your shoes. Avoid packs and straps that do not fit snugly. Loose gear can catch you up or throw you off balance. Secure your glasses with a head strap. Wear proper footwear for rough trails. Wear loose comfortable clothing that will not bind or restrict your safe movement or impede your stepping up or down. Just as you would test-drive a new automobile, try out new shoes, clothing, and gear on short walks near home before depending on them for a full day's outing.

Chapter 7
Easy Walking on Rail Trails

The funding formulas that allow and encourage development of these wonderful rail trails usually are predicated on "shared use" or "mixed use." Trails welcome walkers, bicyclists, and sometimes horseback riders as well. Unfortunately, higher speed bicycles and low-speed walkers and baby strollers often do not mix well. We witness, and have thankfully avoided, many near-collisions due to unwary pedestrians and cyclists alike. Add in the hazards of unpredictable children and dogs, and even the occasional horseback rider…suddenly it's life in the Fast Lane!

Some cyclists and walkers alike have a mindset that this is "their" trail and other parties should accommodate them, whatever way they wander at any speed. As with driving, it's a two-way street and all of us need to exercise more care than usual.

Nearly all trails post safety signage stating that walkers travel on one side and cyclists on the other, except when passing. No universal convention exists to define which side is for walkers. Note the local signage. Don't be that person or group walking or driving on the "wrong side of the road."

When cycling we frequently find groups that split to both sides as we approach, constricting the available lane and funneling both directions of cycle traffic far too closely together. Rather than squeezing between two groups of people, and risk an oncoming bicycle in the mix, we often have to stop.

Some heavily used trails have trained volunteer "ridgerunners" who bicycle or walk the trail as a public safety, mobile bicycle repair, and information resource. These friendly volunteers often have information on historic sites on the trail as well as knowledge about other nearby places to visit.

Rail trails are wonderful resources that we seek out across the country and visit often. Here are our safety tips when using these mixed use trails.

- One side of the trail will usually be designated for walkers, the other side for bikes (which is which seems to vary!) Keep to your designated side of the trail to allow safe passage of bicycles. When you need to stop, stay to the side or step off the trail to make it easier for others to pass.

Stay to the designated side on rail trails

- Cyclists and walkers alike must be prepared to slow or halt their progress, rather than continuing at speed when approaching oncoming groups or when passing groups.

- Keep dogs and children on a short leash (metaphorically, at least for children!). Don't be that person whose dog suddenly stretches his leash all the way across the trail, or whose child darts in front of a bike, causing a crash.

- For bicyclists traveling in the same direction as walkers or other bicyclists, a gentle halloo or short bell ring is common courtesy to offer fellow travelers a warning well before passing them. Having a cheerful-sounding bell on your bike is an added plus.

- Retractable dog leashes lead to poor control; use a six foot leash when bringing your dog on a rail trail.

- Horses follow no written rules. If you encounter horses on the trail, keep quiet, keep to your side, avoid startling movements or loud sounds. Restrain your dog with care. We try to get off the trail completely to allow the infrequent horseback rider safe passage without fear of their horses being spooked. The horses' riders are quite grateful.

- Do not leave dog poop, poop bags, diapers, coffee cups, or wrappers on or near the trail.

- Respect the privacy of abutting houses and landowners.

- Wear reflective gear and use lights at dawn and dusk. Be visible to others.

- Note or photograph safety hazards and email or inform trail maintainers of wash-outs, tree falls, damaged fencing, offensive graffiti, and the like.

- Calmly inform others of your trail safety concerns while not lecturing or confronting.

Chapter 8
Easy Walks Outdoor Programs

Before you head out, look for organizations in your area that can offer outdoor programs and get involved. This is a great way to meet people with shared interests, make new friends, and potentially learn of ways you can give back to your community. Traveling with small groups is also a wonderful way to get more comfortable with spending time on trails, and learning about other opportunities in the area for outdoor experiences.

The following programs I have been involved with have been effective in providing outdoor opportunities for people of various ages and abilities. Grants are sometimes available to help support outdoor events for those with special needs.

> **Outdoor programs bring together people with shared interests**

- Local events on accessible trails—birding, nature, holiday events

- Storywalks® along local trails

- Interpretive Walks, focusing on historical or unique trails and features

- "Make your own storybook" family walks on local trails

- Adaptive bicycling on rail trails

Group walks are challenging, while offering great opportunities for fun when well planned.

Local events on Easy Walk paths

Organizations in many areas often offer public birding and nature walks, and sometimes even arts events. We have attended events that have included a candlelight New Year's Eve walk. These events are usually planned, insured, hosted, and cleaned up afterward by a volunteer committee working with the group that oversees the property. Art events along local rail trails have brought out diverse audiences who might not typically seek out trails, simply to enjoy the art installations.

Storywalks®

Storywalks® can be installed in many locations, both in and outdoors, often along rail trails and other trail systems. We have enjoyed taking children and grandchildren to many of these installations—individual pages of children's books placed on weather-proofed posts. Each page is placed at a distance from the previous page, offering an added incentive to keep moving to learn the rest of the story.

These are great family activities, and can be found across the country. Google "storywalk" and towns near you. Or work with your local library or group overseeing a local trail to create your own Storywalk®.

Interpretive Walks

Walks focusing on natural history as well as historical events abound in our area. I have been blessed with the opportunity to write about, present slide shows, and lead short walks for those interested in local trails featured in my Easy Walks book series. Often this leads to hearing about new places to visit... and new books... and more walks....

"Make Your Own Storybook" walks

A few years ago, a local park ranger and I collaborated to create a program that was accessible to many different populations. We called the program, "Make your own

Partners work together to create a story from adventures on the trail.

storybook" walks. We encouraged participants to partner up during a simple Easy Walk to explore an area, then return to a central meeting place. There we had paper and writing tools ready for participants to create simple "story books" chronicling their experiences, either from reality or from their imagination.

For young, pre-literate children, we encouraged parents to work with their children, enabling each child to dictate their story as the parent wrote down what the child shared. Families with multiple children were offered the help of volunteers who could lend a hand in this task.

Participants with visual impairments were partnered with sighted helpers who could write their experiences down for them. Older children were encouraged to write their story for themselves. Older adults and teens enjoyed creating a story as well. This is a simple concept, limited only by the locations available to make it workable. We offered these programs in every season of the year, and had positive experiences with participants of many ages and abilities during each session.

With our adaptive tandem, Acadia National Park, Maine, Eagle Lake.

This concept is open-ended and adaptable to many different populations, ages, and needs. We share it here in the hopes that it may become a model for others to adapt and make use of.

Adaptive bicycling

Since I have restricted movement in one leg, riding a solo bike is not an option for me. My husband modified (and eventually built from scratch) a tandem bicycle to adapt it to my needs, providing the stability and much of the pedal power we needed. We can now explore lengthy rail trails and often dismount to explore interesting side paths. The bicycle gets me places I could never walk far enough to see!

A google search for adaptive bicycles will reveal an array of specialized solo and tandem bikes, most with three wheels. Some have hand cranks for those whose legs are unable to power a bike. Some of these cycles can be further adapted with an electric motor assist. They are not cheap, but it is sometimes possible to purchase a used one for less.

Participants in an adaptive biking event in Worcester, MA on the Blackstone Bikeway.

I have worked as a volunteer with several organizations that bring specially adapted cycles and kayaks in vans to a location: these are meant to assist people with physical and cognitive challenges and enable them to enjoy an unprecedented opportunity to explore outdoors. Participants have included amputees, war veterans, and those with visual as well as mobility impairments. Witnessing the joy of others regaining movement outdoors has been thrilling.

Part 2
On the Trail with Easy Walks

Chapter 9
Minding Your Manners on Easy Walks

We are social by nature, and with that sociability comes conflict when courtesies are neglected, ignored, or unknown. Trail users have standard courtesies that most try to extend to others. If you are new to spending time outdoors, these "rules" many not seem obvious. Thus, we take the time to list a few here:

- Take only pictures, leave only footprints.

- Take your trash home with you; bring a bag to collect trash while hiking.

- Make way for others using the same trail.

- Avoid shouting except in emergencies.

- Keep your electronic music at home.

- Never toss rocks over a lookout spot.

- Check for restriction notices on dogs before setting out on the trail with your pup.

- Keep your leashed dog a safe distance from others.

- Take your dog's poop with you. Never leave it on the trail for others to deal with.

- Leave rocks on or along the trail in place, unless you are part of a trail maintenance crew.

- Remove fallen tree branches from the trail when possible, and report fallen trees that block trails.

Take only pictures, leave only footprints

"Take only pictures, leave only footprints" is a favored shorthand phrase in the trail community; it reminds visitors to outdoor areas to be respectful of the wildlife that lives there. Plants grow in the area, and views are meant to be enjoyed by all.

> **A "social contract" is needed to keep the peace**

Take your trash with you; bring a collecting bag

Extra points go to those who bring a bag for collecting trash to carry out with them. Refrain from changing the natural landscape with rock towers, scratched signs, or other alterations to the landscape. Remember that others will follow in your footsteps. Adhering to these basic guidelines will put you far ahead of those who are heedless on the trail.

Make way for others

When on a public trail, step to the side to allow others to pass rather than expecting fellow travelers to walk directly behind you. If you are traveling two abreast, step behind your companion to walk in single file to make it easier for others to safely pass you or to pass by you going in the opposite direction. When on a rail trail with more than two in your group, refrain from using the entire trail, with all walking side by side. A passing bike rider may come up on you from behind, and the possibility of injury is real. Do NOT split up on both sides of the trail when encountering others. Choose one side or the other.

> **Do NOT split up on both sides of the trail when encountering others**

Avoid shouting and loud noises except in an emergency

Many people head outdoors seeking the peace and quiet of nature. For these visitors, the outdoors is a sacred space. While we understand the exuberance of children and the joy of burning off excess energy from being cooped up inside, be aware that your behavior on trails, just like in other public spaces, has an impact on others. Loud noises will assuredly scare off any wildlife that visitors might hope to see in the area.

> ## Leave your music home—Listen to the birds

Keep your electronic music at home

Especially when we are visiting rail trails, we notice some bike riders sailing by playing their radios. Perhaps some enjoy this. Most trail users find radio music on the trail to be an intrusion. Likewise, for your part, wearing ear buds for music while walking makes it difficult to hear warnings from bike riders or other walkers coming up behind you. It's important that everyone work together to avoid collisions on the trail.

Never toss rocks over a look-out spot

Children and adults alike casually or joyfully throw rocks over look-outs and break sticks across tree trunks, not considering that there may be hikers, climbers, animals, or geologists below or nearby. Please restrain yourself and others with you.

Check for restrictions on dogs before setting out with a pup

Many of us love dogs and may wish to say hello. Others of us have stability or allergy issues or children who fear

Cliff edges offer the temptation to toss rocks into the abyss. Those on the trails below will not thank you.

dogs and need to keep a distance. Assuming that your dog's approach is always welcome is a poor choice to make on public trails. Keep dogs close at hand and leashed. (See Chapter 10 for more on taking dogs on trails.)

Take your dog's poop with you

No one enjoys finding dog poop left on the trail. A colorful collection of filled dog poop bags along the trail or at the trail head is disturbing. Take it with you, please.

Leave rocks on or along trails unless you are part of a maintenance crew

Bored children (and others) may dig up rocks from a trail surface with innocent intent. They may use the rocks to toss into a nearby pond. Digging up that rock may leave a hole in the trail, creating a tripping hazard. Removing rocks from trails is a job for a trail maintenance crew. If you are motivated, contact the organization that oversees your favorite trail. Volunteers are always needed and welcomed to help perform trail maintenance. Otherwise, leave trail surfaces as they are.

Remove fallen branches from trails when possible

Loose tree branches on trails can be tripping hazards. Shifting them off the path can be a help to others. Fallen trees are usually too large to move and require the expertise of a trail crew to remove them safely without causing more trail damage or leaving unsightly debris. Taking a photo, noting the location as accurately as you can, and contacting the property manager can be helpful.

Chapter 10
Dog Walkers on Easy Walks

Dogs are wonderful. They encourage us to get out to be more active, enhance our quality of life, and have more engagement with other people. We hope that this engagement is always positive! We encourage dog walkers to consider the following:

- Check on whether dogs are allowed before venturing into new areas. Walk your dog where dogs are welcome.

- Use a short six-foot leash while on the trail; longer leashes inhibit control.

- Refrain from letting your dog off-leash on trails where other people are about.

- Don't ruin someone's day; avoid conflicts with other dogs or people. Keep your dog close at hand.

- Be prepared: carry poop bags and clean up! Keep a stash of bags in your car and your pack.

Welcome, canines

Or not. There are so many places to walk. Respect those places that prohibit dogs for the protection of wildlife or for other reasons. Respect leash regulations and do not let your dog off-leash when this is prohibited. Exercise your consideration of other dog walkers, young children, or the physically challenged who do not need the often-unwelcome surprise of your friendly dog rushing at them.

Darting, unleashed dogs and children are a cause of rail trail mishaps. A short leash is necessary to maintain control; retractable leashes are not suitable and have often caused injury to the owner when a dog unexpectedly takes off.

Some trail systems allow dogs off-leash. If your dog does not consistently come when called, keep him or her on a leash. Always keep your dog in sight. If your dog does have an unwelcome encounter with another dog or a person, take steps to control your dog immediately. Apologize, to help defuse this unhappy confrontation.

A *short leash* (six feet or less) is necessary to maintain control

Take your dog's poop with you

The poop fairy is not real! If it were, you would find double your poop back under your pillow. Carry out your dog's goodies in a plastic bag. Do not stealthily sling it off to the side, toss it behind the nearest fence post or tree, or carry it all the way down the trail only to leave it as an offering at the trail head, rather than putting it in your car waste container. Other walkers will unavoidably spot it, to their great dismay. It may eventually melt into the nearest reservoir where you will finally drink it in your local tap water. Or so we've been informed.

Spoiler alert: There is no poop fairy!

Chapter 11
Unexpected Encounters on Easy Walks

Part of the fun and the challenge of getting outdoors is encountering the unexpected. While we have attempted to offer suggestions that will help keep you safe on the trail and enjoy the experience, there is always potential for unexpected encounters. Here are some basic rules of thumb to help you navigate the surprises that may occur while out on the trail.

- Be respectful of lawful ATVs and do not confront.

- Wear blaze-orange to make hunters aware of your presence.

- Avoid confronting strangers in the woods.

- Avoid confronting animals—they have no wish to get close to you.

- Learn about birds and their habits to add extra interest to outdoor visits.

- Set realistic expectations, and prepare for the unexpected.

All-Terrain Vehicles (ATV's) and their riders

These days, ATV riders may well have done much to rediscover and open up old woodland roads, making them more easily accessible. In areas with few trail maintenance volunteers, ATV riders have done some of the same work volunteers might otherwise do in keeping trails clear of shrubbery. Riders may even remove fallen trees that are blocking trails.

ATVs often degrade trails by causing heavy erosion, or creating deep swales, holes, and bog areas. If you encounter a trail with obvious heavy ATV use, it may be best to go elsewhere. The occasional careless or willfully aggressive riders can turn an otherwise pleasant walk into a nasty experience best avoided. In rural areas, ATVs are a common means of local transportation and most riders are responsible.

Wear blaze-orange during hunting season

It is important to recognize the rights of access and historical use of trails by hunters. Most share the same enjoyment of nature as non-hunters, while seeking game. Many state and federal agencies not only allow but promote access by hunters. Hunters often pay these agencies license and game fees, which provide needed funds to help preserve open spaces. Most are safety conscious and diligent about wearing blaze-orange colors.

We should all wear blaze-orange in hunting season. I may be mistaken as a pumpkin with my oversize sweatshirt, hat, and scarf but it's a comfort to me, not to mention the few hunters we encounter, to know we're thinking ahead.

- If you encounter legal hunters on the trail, a simple nod or query is prudent to learn whether they're headed in the same direction you are.

- We occasionally encounter multiple vehicles and hunters at a trailhead. In this case we leave the trail to their use and seek another location where our walking will not conflict with their activities.

- We sometimes notice hunter's "blinds" or "hides" near a trail. Leave these be.

Avoid confronting strangers in the woods

Occasionally we encounter a firepit or old campsite in the woods. On a few occasions we have noticed homeless living sites. While these are mostly either prohibited or ill-advised on public or well-traveled paths, leave them alone and go on by, or turn around if you are uncomfortable. Never interfere with or confront persons at these sites. You can report issues that concern you to local authorities.

Baby otter by the shoreline (Gros Morne, Newfoundland)

Avoid confronting animals and animal hazards

Many of our most treasured and enjoyable outings have been those that have included wildlife sightings. In our years of hikes and Easy Walks, we have rarely and quite memorably encountered snakes, scorpions, skunks, porcupines, black bears, raptors, beavers, otters, harbor seals, a bobcat, elk, antelope, a grizzly bear with cubs, and bison with calves. Some of these animals were next to or smack in the middle of the trail.

If you happen upon animals on a trail, it is best to calmly stop and walk away; wait five or ten minutes to see if the trail is clear before continuing. Do not see how close you can get to these animals to obtain a trophy picture. Do not roll rocks at snakes or yell at the animals. If the animals have not moved, turn around and return the way you came.

Eiders in the Cape Cod Canal in winter, just off the Cape Cod Canal rail trail

The trail will still be there the next time you visit; they probably will not be.

Field guides or phones can help identify birds

Learn about bird habitats

Beach and field areas may be seasonally closed to protect nesting birds, turtles, or other wildlife. Keep dogs leashed to avoid encroaching on these areas.

We enjoy observing migrating waterfowl seasonally every spring and fall as they visit the lake near where we live. Our visits to shoreline beaches often offer opportunities to witness the feeding behavior of waterfowl in the area. We have witnessed several bald eagles soaring over trees in a group, hoping to catch by surprise the seagulls, eider ducks, buffleheads, and mergansers floating just off shore.

We are not bird experts, we're simply among the many who enjoy seeing birds and observing their behavior in the wild. A basic field guide, or phone with internet access will provide a wealth of information to help you identify birds you see in your travels. Before long, you may start to recognize familiar birds as old friends. It's all part of the adventure.

Set realistic expectations, be prepared for the unexpected

Most wild animals are intensely aware of our presence and tend to make themselves scarce when they hear us approaching. On our outings we focus on plants, weather, historical land use, interesting bridge and culvert constructions, geology, interesting landforms, and more. Those times we see wildlife are then a wonderful surprise!

Part 3
Enabling Easy Walks

Chapter 12
Skills for Leading Easy Walks

Group leaders can help create great outdoor experiences. Leading a group whose members are of considerably different ages, abilities and stamina, and those who are differently-abled can be challenging. Before heading out when you are leading such groups, consider these tips:

- Always check the weather forecast before setting out.

- Take into account the type of trail, any challenges, and the abilities of your group's weakest members. Are they reasonably well matched or should you consider a different trail or a shorter outing?

- Appoint a "sweep" before you go—a person who will stay at the rear of the group to ensure that no stragglers are unaided or left behind.

- When leading children, or those with special needs, assigning "buddy" partners can help keep participants engaged.

- Understand any health issues in the group—bee allergies, bad knees, disabilities, and so on. Know the possible warning signs of trouble as well as how to respond.

- Ask those with special needs to help you understand what is helpful and how you can respectfully assist on the trail, particularly if there are balance or stamina issues.

- Build in opportunities to rest, eat, and drink, especially for children and those with less stamina.

- Prepare to assist children or adults who may need to answer the call of nature. Help them avoid peeing near waterways or on trails.

- Scout ahead when unsure of trail conditions. The group needs to follow the decisions of the leader.

- If lost, either attempt to backtrack or stay put for safety.

- Be prepared to change plans (or even shorten the walk) due to weather, trail conditions, exhaustion or health issues, or other unexpected situations. Leave your walkers wanting more. There will almost always be another chance to return.

Check the weather

The best-made plans can be quickly ruined by threatening weather. As a group leader, the person in charge is responsible for the group. If a storm is coming your way, the safety of the group comes first, even if it means disappointing participants. Be prepared.

> **Successful group leaders anticipate problems before they occur**

Prepare the group before setting out on the trail

The most successful group leaders anticipate problems before they occur. Rather than waiting for people to do things that are unsafe, set ground rules at the beginning, making clear any safety concerns participants need to be aware of.

Appoint a "sweep" before you go

Especially if you are going out with multiple children, older adults, or those with special needs, have someone accept responsibility for staying at the back of the group to assure that no one is left behind or requires assistance.

Buddies

Pairing off participants before heading out is a helpful tool for sharing the responsibility of keeping everyone safe on the trail. With younger children the initial pairing may be problematic. Do not hesitate to step in to shift buddies if needed.

Health issues? Ask before heading out

Many children and adults have hidden health issues that could become an emergency on the trail. Be respectful of privacy, while doing what you can to be prepared in case of a medical emergency while on the trail.

Does anyone in the group wear a medic-alert bracelet? Do you know what it is for and what you need to do in an emergency? Do you have access to band-aids, cold packs, and other emergency kit items? Depending on your group, you may want to designate one responsible person to carry a kit of this type for you. It may sound overly cautious, especially if you have a group of walkers you are not well-acquainted with, and you may someday be glad you brought these items along.

If you are the one with special needs, communicate those needs to the person you are going with on the trail, or to the group leader.

Other concerns? Special needs?
Know before you go

You may have a participant who is fearful of dogs. A child may react strongly to loud noises. You cannot prepare for everything. If possible, learn about these concerns to be in a better position to respond appropriately if the need arises.

Those with bad knees, balance issues, or other challenges still can experience joy in getting outdoors.

Handicaps do not prevent feeling joy in the outdoors

As with children and older adults, supporting those with physical mobility challenges, with visual, hearing, and cognitive impairments, or with other challenges, requires preparation. Choose wisely about where to walk. Scouting out in advance a trail, park, cemetery, or other outdoor destination is always helpful. While not always possible to completely check out an area, it may be helpful to slow your group down by taking a few minutes to scope out the lay of the land before continuing on a trail.

The more challenges participants have, the more support (additional volunteers) will be needed. Do not feel you must eliminate all but the most established (i.e., paved) trails if you are hoping to introduce children or adults with special needs to the outdoors. Many hands make for a more positive experience. Some woodland trails can be wide, fairly smooth, and can offer wonderful surprises along the way. The resulting walk may not feel "easy" for the responsible leaders; that's part of accepting responsibility for the group, even if it is simply your special needs child, or a small group of special needs adults.

When working with participants who are visually impaired, it is helpful to understand how to convey information. Directions may need to be provided differently. Ask participants how you can be most helpful. Find out in advance if a walking partner is needed. As with any group, a buddy system works well for visually impaired participants too. Make time to allow visually impaired participants to take in their surroundings, offer visual descriptions for what they can sense yet are not able to see, and ask how else you can help them enjoy the experience.

Plans may change—let participants know in advance

Leave them wanting more— Plan a smaller loop, or turn back sooner

The outdoors can offer excitement and wonder, and can also be unpredictable. Regardless of how much we prepare, the weather can change, or someone may fall ill or become injured. The trail you planned to travel on may have been washed out and the group forced to turn back. Traveling with a group means that a trail that might be great for some may turn out not to be appropriate for all. Knowing in advance that they may have to adapt will not change how participants feel if their hopes are dashed. Begin the conversation prior to setting out, reminding them that we cannot control nature. It's part of the joy, and part of the challenge.

Turning a sloping rock face into a slide. (Hopedale Parklands, Hopedale, MA)

Leave them wanting more

Plan a smaller loop than you might wish, or turn back sooner than your walking partners think you should. When you get back, participants will either be glad you stopped when you did, or else they will ask, "When can we come back?" Either response is a win.

Allow time for rest

Do not head back out as soon as the last of the group arrives at a certain point on the trail. This will deny those slower walkers the chance to catch their breath. You will likely have a group with people of different skill levels and differing stamina. Be clear that you plan to leave no one behind, that the group needs to stay together, and that everyone deserves the chance to rest. It's all part of being considerate and creating a safe environment for all participants. During these rest stops, be sure everyone can take a drink of water, pull out a snack, and have the chance to eat if they wish.

> **Older adults have life experience, but may not have challenged their bodies recently. Respect is key.**

Walking with children

We learn by experimenting. Trying out a new place is a risk with many potential rewards. If you have particularly adventuresome children, visit the designated park or trail yourself before bringing energetic little ones with you. Wide open fields offer great delights and wonders for young and old. Birds love open spaces, as do butterflies and other wildlife. Wider carriage roads offer clear sight lines to keep children more easily in view.

Setting expectations goes double for outings with children. The expectations do not have to be onerous. Setting clear limits is a kindness to children often determined to push the boundaries. Being aware of your surroundings and mindful of places to avoid (like steep drop-offs and other hazards) can help prevent unnecessary emergencies or outright danger.

Practice listening skills prior to your initial outing. When you call, do the children in your group respond? Do not just keep calling. Get up and make sure the children respond.

Walking with older adults

As we age, our balance, strength, energy, and weather tolerances diminish. We may not realize these limits until taxed on the trail. Be prepared to rest more or turn around earlier.

The call of nature

Never permit a walker to pee directly on a trail. Avoid areas close to rivers or streams or ponds—pee can travel and contaminate waterways. If the person in your party must defecate, do your best to dig a hole and bury it far off the trail and far from any waterways. Cover well with dirt and leaves. Never walk away and leave a pile of paper and refuse for others to find.

Everyone "goes"
Be prepared

Ask an adult, child, or person with special needs if they need help. Suggest the best location for them to relieve themselves, and stay nearby if they need assistance. Scope out the area first and avoid the often ubiquitous poison ivy or poison oak on both ground and trees.

Scout ahead if unsure of the trail

When on an unfamiliar trail, have one experienced person scout ahead if you're uncertain of wayfinding. If you're unable to see a clear way forward, backtrack. When taking forks on the trail, stop and look behind you to imprint what the trail will look like upon your return.

> **When encountering intersections, look back to see where you've been**

Regardless of the decision to go on or turn back, do not split up. Splitting up makes it more difficult for anyone trying to locate the group to find all of you if you are lost. If you are really confused, stay put. Otherwise, you risk tiring out everyone and making your group more difficult to track down.

Tell others your plans before you go

Did you remember to tell someone else where you were going and when to expect you back? Do you have cell phone service where you are? Most of us have felt lost at one time or another when outside walking. Did you bring a map of the area with you? Are there nearby roads marked on the map? Maps and local roads can be important for reaching help. Do not hesitate to head to a visible house and ask for directions. Can you hear cars in the distance? Did you bring water for each person? Snacks? Extra clothes? All these steps will increase your chances of keeping your companions safe and getting to the help you need sooner rather than later in the case of an emergency.

Our hope is that you never need to put this information to use. Staying on marked trails and bringing a map with you of the area you are walking in are all safeguards against getting lost in the first place. Cell phone coverage, while not a fail-safe backup, can offer an option to get help if truly needed.

Chapter 13
Trail Stewardship for Easy Walks

This chapter is directed to trail maintainers and constructors. Those of us looking for Easy Walks are greatly impacted by trails that have been laid out with ease of access in mind. We have learned to be on the lookout for stair railings that do not offer safe support. We often can survey a trail before going too far to judge if it has too many trip hazards. While most trails will not be handicapped accessible, many trails can be made more accessible for a wider range of visitors with some thoughtful choices of surface materials, hand rails, and elimination of steps.

Many land stewards and their organizations are run by volunteers. Those who maintain and build local trails do amazing work, yet may not be aware of what constitutes a challenge to those needing Easy Walks. Fortunately a number of professional organizations—Appalachian Mountain Club (AMC), Adirondack Mountain Club (ADK), the National Park Service (NPS), and the US Forest Service (USFS)—have carefully developed guidance on building and maintaining trails. Seek out these references (links at the end of this chapter) before undertaking changes to signage or relocating trails.

Eagle Scouts are responsible for many trail improvement projects throughout the U.S. Supporting an Eagle Scout candidate will require an investment of time. The benefit to your community can be great. We encourage local land stewards to work with Eagle Scout candidates to improve trail accessibility within your communities. We hope the following information will be of use toward that goal.

Some challenges to what might otherwise be Easy Walk trails may force some to turn around or avoid the trail altogether. They can include:

- Too many roots, rocks, or slopes

- Fallen trees that cannot be stepped over or around

- Severe erosion, washouts, or eroded waterbars that lead to impassible heights and flooded areas

- Overheight, that is, too tall stone or wood steps

- Missing, damaged, or over-large hand railings

- Confusing or missing signage

- Overhanging or ingrown poison ivy that cannot be easily avoided

- Slippery or overly narrow wooden "bog bridges"

- Fall hazards—cliffs, pits, unstable slopes

What can we all do to make new and existing trails more accessible? We encourage readers who experience challenges on specific trails to get in touch with the land stewards of the trails you enjoy to offer your experience. Your feedback can help make a difference for others who will visit an area in the future. Keep it positive and remember to express appreciation for those who do the work of looking after these properties.

Here are some suggestions specifically for those who are willing to take on the challenge of building and maintaining local trails, to make those trails more accessible:

Wayfinding and signage

Too often we see familiar trails damaged or ruined by new, careless, or ad-hoc application of painted markings everywhere of various unclear sizes and muddled clarity.

Sturdy plastic colored markers of consistent shape can be purchased or easily made from vinyl folder materials and loosely nailed to trees at appropriately distant intervals.

Paint cannot be modified! Stick to loosely nailed markers on trees and posts. (The use of painted markings on treeless rocky trails requires careful planning and execution, as formulated by the AMC.)

Implement clear, consistent and appropriate trail markers. Refer to published trail manuals for guidelines that illustrate what is clear and not excessively overt, and that avoids tree damage. Sturdy plastic colored markers of consistent shape can be purchased or easily made from vinyl folder materials, and loosely nailed (not flush with the bark) to trees at appropriately distant intervals. (Not every other tree...)

Other additions to make a trail more inviting include:

- Large-format laminated maps at trail kiosks offer visitors an overview of their trail choices along with features or hazards before starting out. These are a great help.

- Inform visitors of any restrictions or conditions before they start out via appropriate signage: seasonal visitation, wildlife protection, hunting permissions, and so on.

- Dogs: Are they allowed? Must they be leashed?

- Do certain trails have unusual fall hazards, such as at quarries, mineshafts, or cliffs? Help the walker decide which trails may not be appropriate.

- Are certain features, plants, or fish protected under historic or state and federal statutes?

Parking

Visitors to trails you oversee may ask themselves these questions: "That looks like a well-used, unmarked trailhead or trail access point. Can I park here without getting stuck? Will I be towed? Will my car be here when I get back?"

Put yourself in the place of those with mobility challenges who are preparing to set out on what for them may be a challenging outing on your Easy Walk trail. Trailheads at publicly owned or publicly accessible spaces are worth designating clearly. Even a small sign will suffice. Some owners post a written limit on the number of spaces. Good relations with the neighbors or town may dictate posting No Parking signs beyond designated limits. Seasonal restrictions may apply during mud season, icy conditions, or hunting seasons.

Improved trail surfaces

Trail surfaces should not be "improved" from their seemingly natural look, without careful planning and with the consensus of owners, maintainers, and users. Trails for walkers and/or bicyclists should be packed down and not feature loose materials.

Good materials to add to trail surfaces include:

- Stone dust is ideal for most surfaces.

- Highway-specific "dense grade" is a mixture of stone dust and small angular crushed stones, never rounded rocks. The mix of sizes allows it to pack down well and build up a thicker smooth surface, preferred for heavy use and bicycling.

- 3/8" diameter crushed stone, not rounded "river rock" or "bank run gravel" which will not compact. 3/4" diameter crushed stone will not wash away as easily but can be harder to walk on and quite sharp to sit on or fall on. Larger 1-1/2" or 3" diameter stone is unsuitable for trails.

- Clean wood chips, free of dyes and invasives may be used away from streams. Use is discouraged in some areas due to the impact on streams or plants.

- Serious trail crews such as on the Appalachian Trail seek to re-create a "natural" look while improving hazardous or erosion-prone areas. This may include ferrying in local dirt, small rocks, and outright heavy construction with flat and pinned stones. Dirt and stone "borrow pits" are situated out of sight and carefully refurbished and brushed over.

Surface materials to avoid:

- Scrutinize "clean fill" that may be contaminated with asphalt, concrete, or other debris.

- Never use those "free" asphalt millings waste which local contractors may be eager to donate. In addition to leaching oils into the woods and streams, their rounded consistent shape means they never pack down and are a walking, and particularly a bicycling, hazard, as well as being unsightly.

Playgrounds and a few select ADA (Americans with Disabilities) trails may feature Rubber Crumb surfaces. These are unsightly and not appropriate for woodland trails.

Bridges and Stairs

Even the best Easy Walk trail is likely to cross water, climb a hill, or need to manage runoff.

Bridges can be simple and need careful construction to ensure they are stable, feature a low step on and low step off (or a ramp to facilitate handicapped accessibility), and have suitable full-length railings that can be gripped by hand.

Bog bridges are boards or chain sawn half-logs laid atop crossmembers to span boggy trail sections. Smooth surfaces quickly become slippery from rain, ice, and organics. AMC and other guidelines require rough irregular surfaces, flush or recessed fasteners, and adequate widths. Single or double boards can create a high-wire balancing act for some walkers. Three-board widths are preferable to two.

Water bars are wood or stone "steps" carefully trenched crossways into the trail on steep slopes, to divert water off the trail. Building water bars is a lot of work and must be done appropriately and carefully, otherwise they may pose hazards or quickly fail.

Because of the tremendous effort needed to find or make water bar materials, dig trenches, set and pin them, and backfill them, they are invariably spaced too far apart. As the trail eventually erodes the water bars become giant steps, impassable for those with mobility challenges. Appropriate spacing and stepping height must be carefully planned. Many popular trails in the White Mountains have eroded several feet deep, creating a hazardous rock scrambling experience rather than a hike or walk.

Steps and stairs are an important aid to moving along steep slopes or changes in elevation. All too often, a handy rock or chain sawn log section is rolled into place as a step, regardless of height or stability, leading to a surprise giant step. Use the residential buildings code as a guide: keep step height to roughly six inches, and step depth to no less than twelve inches.

Step and stair railings. Railings all too often stop short of the top or bottom of a set of stairs, reducing their usefulness. Whether one is mobility-impaired or simply carrying a child or a heavy pack, a usable and continuous railing is needed, at least 8" beyond the limits of the top and bottom stairs.

Barrier and fencing material choices are very important

- Use 2-3/8" diameter wood and steel railings mounted on offset hangers (metal brackets that allow for solid hand grip around the railing) in accordance with ADA codes for accessibility. Cost and aesthetics preclude using these in most woodland situations, but if a trailhead features a steep access stair, it may be the best choice.

- Many trails feature standard dimensional lumber for railings: a 2x6 is 1-1/2" wide. Use finished, planed lumber, not "rough" lumber from the sawmill. While users can run their hand along the top, this is still not graspable. On steep stairs, 2-3/8" diameter railings should be mounted inboard of the lumber railing structure.

Barrier fencing: Many rail trails have frequent barriers at slopes and wetlands to protect trail visitors from stumbling down slopes. Cost is a driving consideration in choice of materials and systems.

The exhausting work of digging fence-post holes often leads to shallow and poorly set posts. It's best to rent a two-handed, gas-powered post-hole auger at your local construction rental store. Best practice is to cement posts in place, returning later to hide the exposed cement with local "duff" or leaf and soil materials.

Material choice is often budget-driven

- Plastic lumber is hardly natural looking, yet may be the best choice for durability, long-term cost-effectiveness, and splinter-free usage.

- Pressure-treated wood may last and is unsightly and splintery.

- Untreated, planed dimensional lumber will be less splintery and will rot quickly.

- Treated wood, cedar, or stone posts with multiple rope railings or stainless wire rope railings are appropriate in some settings. A single rope is never appropriate. Round and split posts may look rustic, are usually loosely set, and become a maintenance challenge as they come apart or are vandalized.

- Some quite wonderful local rail trails feature tropical hardwood railings fastened with stainless hardware. They will last a long time, look great, and are certainly not cheap nor environmentally sustainable.

Trail maintenance

Maintenance is required to keep a trail to the standards of an Easy Walk. Scheduled trail walks ("ridgewalking") by a responsible volunteer can determine needs and plan removal of light obstacles. Most organizations rely on volunteer labor, perhaps with a coordinator on assignment or stipend. "Adopt-a-trail" programs are frequently implemented.

If your trailhead features a kiosk and sign-in book, encourage visitors to note any maintenance needs. Common needs can include:

- Removal of fallen trees (requiring chainsaw, safety gear, and poison ivy safeguards)

- Light clearing of ingrowth, brush, and fallen branches

- Trash removal

- Maintenance of wayfinding and trailhead signage

- Parking area snowplowing and maintenance

- Removal of poison ivy. Casual trail visitors may not be aware of or able to recognize poison ivy. Especially on heavily traveled areas, remove poison ivy that is overhanging the trail or growing into walkways.

These maintenance tasks can be formally arranged or accomplished by a responsible committee or trail adopter.

Please avoid the following:

- Avoid "volunteering" your ad-hoc changes or supplements to trail markings, however much you believe they are incomplete or lacking. Inform a trail committee or owner if there are significant issues. Trail markings should be implemented to AMC recommended practices, by informed persons. It is unpleasant to be confronted with violently colored spray painted blazes on every other tree.

- To our amazement, in one local region, several persons annually venture out on trails in the fall with gas-powered leaf blowers, to clear "hazardous" leaves and enable folks to see where they are stepping. The piercing din, gasoline fumes, and resultant eroding trails are damaging to the trail system and are both disturbing (and truly anathema) to the enjoyment of the outdoors. We do not have the right to modify trails for our own personal desires; consider the common good and the practices of the landowner or legal steward.

- Please do not attempt ad-hoc trail changes, to bar off or fill in natural and historic features that may seem hazardous to you. These can include historic foundations, natural rock shelters, mine adits (surface openings to historic mines), cliffs, or water features. Refer to AMC and other agencies' recommended practices for the location and type of natural wood barrier or signage, when appropriate.

- Avoid chopping and hacking trees and branches that are "in the way" of a more convenient view or stream crossing. Such changes should be carefully planned, with consideration for long-term plans for an area, erosion changes, and the like.

- Rock "temples" and other artful constructions are not natural. Enjoy the trail and "Leave Only Footprints."

Trail maintenance and construction resources:

Sustainable Mountain Trails Sketchbook

nps.gov/orgs/1804/upload/SustainableMountainTrail sSketchbook-COTI_2006.pdf

AMC Field Guide to Trail Building and Maintenance, 2nd ed.

amazon.com/Field-Guide-Trail-Building Maintenance/ dp/0910146306

AMC Trail Adopters Handbook

americantrails.org/images/documents/FAQ_ AMCadopt.pdf

United States Forest Service Trail Construction and Maintenance Notebook

(fs.fed.us/t-d/pubs/htmlpubs/htm07232806/page02. htm)

Environmental Considerations in Trail Design

alexmckenzie.weebly.com/trail-design-construction-maintenance.html

Note from the Author

As a single parent at age 30, I sought out people to head outdoors with me and my children. Local Massachusetts Audubon group walks became a great resource and guide for our family. I often enlisted friends to join us on these outings.

Sudden illness in my mid-30s robbed me of my ability to walk. While I was healing and regaining a measure of mobility, I longed to get back outdoors. Short walks to a nearby lake offered challenge, healing, and comfort. With friends and family I began to take Easy Walks, even though I didn't use this term at the time.

When I remarried, my husband, an experienced hiker, introduced me to hiking poles for balance, along with strategies to make more challenging trails possible. Our search for interesting and accessible walks led to documenting locations, which eventually became my *Easy Walks in Massachusetts* book series. Our weekends today often feature local travel outdoors, occasional long vacations, and always a search for Easy Walks wherever we are!

Drawing from my experience in self-publishing as a professional personal historian, I have authored several books in the *Easy Walks in Massachusetts* trail guide series, all available on Amazon.

This latest book, *Finding Easy Walks Wherever You Are*, distills our experiences looking for Easy Walks and making them safe and enjoyable under various circumstances. My hope is that you will find helpful tools and checklists in this book to assist your search for trails and safe enjoyment outdoors. Happy Trails!

Marjorie Turner Hollman
MarjorieTurner.com
July 2020

Acknowledgments

- Sue Stephenson for proofreading, book design, and cover design and cover photo.

- Francie King, my extraordinary editor. Any mistakes in the final book are mine, not hers.

- Early and later draft readers, Amy Bartelloni, Carol Bird, Alida Santandrea, Jennifer Powell, Sue Stephenson, Mary Glen Chitty, Christine Doyle, Marcy Marchello, Devon Lucas, John Murzycki, Anne Parker, Pat Marcotte, and the Bellingham book group.

- My husband Jon, for making years of Easy Walks possible, for developmental editing, and for chapters on Rail Trail safety and Trail Stewardship.

- Mark Mandeville and Raianne Richards for encouragement and a generous Foreword. Their Massachusetts Walking Tours are an inspiration! Please seek out their tours and concerts.

- Kathryn Parent, for collaborating with me to create the "Make your own storybook" walk series, mentioned in Chapter 8, Easy Walks Programs.

- Heartfelt thanks to many companions, including my children and grandchildren, who have generously walked at my slow pace and volunteered to help investigate new trails with me, just for fun, as well as for my *Easy Walks in Massachusetts* books, available on Amazon.